Divorce to Healing

*31 Days of
Healing and Wholeness*

By Brent D Papineau

Copyright © 2016 Brent D Papineau
All rights reserved
ISBN: 1530366364
ISBN-13: 978-1530366361

Contents

Contents by Subject	xi
Acknowledgements	xiii
About This Book	xv
Introduction	1
Day 1: Shock	7
Day 2: Identity	9
Day 3: Blame	11
Day 4: Anger	13
Day 5: Obedience	15
Day 6: Choices	17
Day 7: Loneliness	19
Day 8: Perspective	21
Day 9: Trust	23
Day 10: Forgiveness	25
Day 11: Thankfulness	27
Day 12: Confusion	29
Day 13: Acceptance	31
Day 14: Feelings	33
Day 15: Bitterness	35
Day 16: Pain	37

Day 17: Yearning	39
Day 18: Baggage	41
Day 19: Grief	43
Day 20: Boundaries	45
Day 21: Hope	47
Day 22: Comparison	49
Day 23: Regret	51
Day 24: Trusting	53
Day 25: Responsibility	55
Day 26: Patience	57
Day 27: Reconciliation	59
Day 28: Shame	61
Day 29: Evidence	63
Day 30: Peace	65
Day 31: Joy	67
Next Steps	69
Verses	71

Contents by Subject

Acceptance	31
Anger	13
Baggage	41
Bitterness	35
Blame	11
Boundaries	45
Choices	17
Comparison	49
Confusion	29
Evidence	63
Feelings	33
Forgiveness	25
Grief	43
Hope	47
Identity	9
Joy	67
Loneliness	19
Obedience	15
Pain	37
Patience	57

Peace	65
Perspective	21
Reconciliation	59
Regret	51
Responsibility	55
Shame	61
Shock	7
Thankfulness	27
Trust	23
Trusting	53
Yearning	39
Next Steps	69
Verses	71

Acknowledgements

First and foremost, I want to give all glory, honor, and praise to God the Father, His only begotten Son and my Lord and Savior, Jesus Christ, and the Holy Spirit through which I exist and am able to have life and do anything. Words will never express my feelings, and I will walk with them all the days of my life doing everything I can to let them live through me to bless and love others.

Indescribable love and thanks to my wife, Christy Papineau, who without her full support every day I have known her, would cause this life to be so much less blessed and enjoyable. She is the strongest, most sacrificial, forgiving, thoughtful, and precious person, let alone woman, I have ever been blessed to know. Anything and everything I am today is because of God blessing me with just one more day with her. I love you, baby!!

Thanks to Joshua and Victoria, my children and legacy. May you know how much I love you and that God loves you so much more than your mom and I could ever love you. Go and be all He has called you to be.

Thanks to my brother and his wife, Dave and Regan Papineau, for being there for me through all the tough times and loving me despite all my failures. Without you, I would not be able to minister to others in this way.

Thanks to my sister, Traci Papineau, for helping bring forth these words through her gift of editing and writing while also preserving the heart God gave me to help others.

Thanks to my dad and mom, Russell and Ethyl Papineau, for loving me through all of my failures while also demonstrating that love means staying faithful and supportive through every season in life. I pray that I can be as strong and loving as you as I continue to lead my family.

Thanks to all of my pastors, friends, and group members with whom I have been blessed to go through life. Through you I have been able to bless others through ministry.

Thanks to all of you, for trusting me with your life enough to speak life to you through these words.

Be blessed!!

About This Book

When God gave me the thought for this devotional, I felt that it needed to have a little different scope and usage than a regular devotional book.

First, I wanted something that could be used or started on any day of the month and you would be able to start connecting. Every day is different and I think the concept of days versus chapters made a lot more sense.

Second, I wanted to be able to present it in such a way that it could be used over and over again. The title is not 31 days **_TO_** or **_FOR_** Healing and Wholeness, because we all know that it is a process and just doing a 31 day devotional will not do it for you.

Third, I wanted to be able to have a resource that people felt comfortable with using as a measuring stick. By going through the 31 days multiple times, you can see your progress pertaining to each subject. Maybe this month you have no desire to forgive, but within a month or two, it may be something you are willing to address.

Fourth, I wanted a resource that people could pick up at any time and refer back to it, especially since the contents have also been listed by subjects to make it easy to find that specific area you desire to read about.

Lastly, I wanted something that people would be willing to use and borrow or give away so that it would bless others as well. There are millions of hurting people, just in America, that would love to have something to refer to when they are needing a little extra help.

My prayer is that this devotional will be a blessing to help you heal, become whole, and be able to help someone else through what God is doing in you.

Introduction

"Jesus and I are movin' on!!"

    It was during a counseling session with my pastor and associate pastor in a small office in a small church where God gave me the statement that would carry me during the worst days of my life.

    Looking back, I was still a baby in my walk with God. Even though I had been saved a few years before and did my best to gain wisdom through going to church and hanging out with the right people, I found myself trying to hang on with all I had.

    The divorce papers were served on the day that OJ Simpson was found not guilty in the murder of his wife and her friend. The one thing I really remember that day was the thought that he was found not guilty and I was found guilty of having to serve his sentence through divorce.

Now I can see how my inability to communicate my feelings, even on a basic level, led to issues in our marriage. I did everything I could to reconcile and in the end, she just wanted out.

Thank God I had my brother, Dave, and his family along with my church family to help me during that time. As a Christian, striving to be more like Jesus every day, it was the flesh and bone hands and feet of those around me who loved me through my struggles.

What my brother Dave did for me was exactly what I needed. He told me that he loved me and would be there for me anytime, anyplace, and for any reason. He also said he was not going to be all up in my business about it, but to come to him when I needed him.

My dad is a wonderful man who raised us boys to be rather self-sufficient. In so many ways, it has allowed me to figure things out on my own, thus learning through trial and error. It worked, to a point.

What they did was to give me the space to figure it out on my own while providing the support I wanted when I was ready. But I needed more, so much more.

That more was Jesus!! I had to fill in all the space with the love, grace, and mercy that only God could give me. I was saved, yet I needed to allow Him to guide and lead me, and heal me to make me whole again.

The best example of this was one night when I felt discouraged and beat down. I figured I needed to spend some time with Dave and his family. Guess what? They decided to head out of town to get away for a couple of days and I didn't know they had left.

I walked back to my dingy apartment and cried more tears that night than I ever had before or ever will again. I needed my brother, my best friend. I needed ...... God!!

Looking back, it was the best thing in my healing process. I needed to get to the point of total desperation. I needed to hit rock bottom. And I did!!

What did God do? He used who I thought was my strength (Dave) to show me that only God is my true strength. Fully and completely, I received God as the only answer to all of my needs.

My introductory statement above was something God told me before in that small church office. I finally knew, deep down in my soul, what it means to walk with Jesus.

Fast forward a few years, I was now living in another town and guess what? Yes, it happened AGAIN!!!

Divorce #2. What just happened, and now what? I trusted God and did everything right, I thought, but yet again, I was facing the tragedy of divorce.

After only a few months of marriage, I was faced again with questioning my foundational relationship with God. This time, I was prepared. Yet after two and a half years of trying to reconcile my marriage, it was over.

But God was there for me every step of the way. Dave and his family had moved, but I had a relationship with God now that was a firm foundation, unmovable and unshakable. Even though the enemy did his best to cause me to stumble, my God was faithful and held me in His arms through it all.

Now you may be wondering why I am telling you all of this. Well, I want to encourage you that God loves you and wants you to be blessed, even through your toughest and most difficult struggles.

After my second divorce was final, I immediately called my boss to tell him I was moving and had decided to transfer with the company. I wanted to become involved with an amazing church in Jacksonville, Florida and to join their worship team. God had something awesome for me, but I did not know how awesome, until I let go and let God lead me.

I met Dave at his work the moment I rolled into town and we went to lunch. He told me the worship team was having a little worship time as part of a huge New Year's Eve party, the very next day.

That night I met my wife, Christy. She was a member of the worship team and close friends with Dave and his family. God was up to something. Within 17 days, we went on our first date and were married less than 9 months later.

We have now been happily married for over 12 years and have 2 wonderful children. Together we have helped hundreds of people in various marriage and divorce groups while serving in other leadership roles at Celebration Church of Jacksonville, FL.

And we know that God causes all things to work together for good to those who love God, to those who are called according to His purpose. Romans 8:28

My point in telling you my story is not to tell you that everything will work out for you like it did for me. I wanted to share what God did for me and what He can and will do for you, *if* you let Him. God gave me a foundation of peace and wisdom that led me to healing and wholeness in Him.

Divorce to Healing: Day 1
Shock

Words will never be able to describe how you are feeling. "What just happened? How? When? WHY?"

When you first hear those words "I want a divorce" or are blind-sided by papers served to you when you least expect it, no words do it justice. Feelings that you have never experienced before are flooding over you. You can't even get the words out because… "WHAT JUST HAPPENED?"

At this time, you are filled with every emotion and a million thoughts that race through your mind. It is a time when you need to just stop and gather yourself. Even though you may just want to do something crazy and ask for forgiveness later, don't do it!! Just stop, drop (to your knees), and roll (to the foot of the cross)!!

No advice at this moment will do you any good until you realize that there are things going on that you cannot control. There are things going on that need to be analyzed from a higher vantage point.

There will come a time when the feelings of shock will be gone and other feelings form. Don't allow negative feelings to control your actions or reactions.

When you are in distress and all these things have come upon you, in the latter days you will return to the L ORD *your God and listen to His voice. Deuteronomy 4:30*

Right now, the only one who understands what you are feeling and going through, is God. He is the only one who can give you peace for your today and your future.

<u>Prayer</u>
God, I have no idea what is going on, but I choose to trust You. I need You now to show me the way. Please bring forth Your true Word, in Jesus' name. Amen.

Divorce to Healing: Day 2
Identity

How many times have you filled your mind with thoughts that you know, deep down, are not true? Have you ever felt totally unsure of who you are just because you are separated or divorced?

The person you are has nothing to do with the events and situations that happen to you. Bankruptcy, strained friendships, and job loss may happen, but you are still you. It does not change who you are. It may force you to change and adapt, but it should not change your identity.

You are not what happens to you; you are the result of how you react to what happens to you.

As devastating as divorce is, you can move forward and grow through it. How you handle every situation from now on is a choice. Make it a positive choice.

A divorce may change how you have to adapt in life to move forward, but it does not change the fact that you are a person that can and will rise above whatever is in front of you.

Know that God doesn't make junk, and you are a treasure to the One who has created everything.

"Before I formed you in the womb I knew you, before you were born I set you apart..." Jeremiah 1:5a NIV

You are a unique, special, one-of-a-kind creation from God. You are a sum total of what God says about you, not what others or your self-image may say about you.

<u>Prayer</u>
God, help me to remember that you created me and that you love me for who I am. I am your child and may my identity be wrapped in you today, in Jesus' name. Amen.

Divorce to Healing: Day 3
Blame

One of the easiest things to do in life is to blame the other person. Dropping a pass on the football field, causing that business report to be late, or describing your failed marriage can be explained many different ways.

No matter what happened, just acknowledge that all people make mistakes. When it comes to your relationship, some mistakes can be more visible than others. Even if you are the only one who seems to be trying to do the right things, blaming someone else for all of the failure in a marriage is just not fair, or correct.

Does it mean they are off the hook? Does it mean they should not be held accountable? Are you 100% innocent in everything you have said and done? If you are being honest, no.

Taking the emotions out of dealing with any sin that affected the marriage and led to a divorce is one of the biggest hurdles for people. Emotions can turn facts into weapons of undesirable destruction.

There are always two sides to every story: your side and the wrong side. Well, maybe not, but it sure feels that way.

Don't spend your time blaming the other party. Spend time understanding your shortcomings and how you can overcome them as you move forward.

Every man's way is right in his own eyes, but the LORD *weighs the hearts. Proverbs 21:2*

Don't let the facts control your emotions. Let the facts stand alone.

<u>*Prayer*</u>
God, help me to see that I can let the facts be shown for what they are. May I know my faults and help me change what I need to change, in Jesus' name. Amen.

Divorce to Healing: Day 4
Anger

One of the first and most destructive emotions that is experienced in any failing marriage is anger. Believe me, you probably have a perfectly good reason to go off on your husband or wife. They cheated, abused, abandoned, or destroyed that which no one has a right to destroy. You have the facts and it is time to let it out!!

Let me help reign yourself in. As much as you have a right to blow up, is it the best thing for you to do right now? Are you in a volatile situation? Are the children near you? Would you be in danger if you just let them have it?

You have every reason to be angry, but righteous anger is still just that; anger. There comes a time when you must heal from the pain of the hurt and learning to process the anger you feel is a large piece of the healing puzzle.

Some people will bottle things up and then explode. Others may just live a life of being resentful because they have not worked through it. Wherever you are at on the anger scale, do not hesitate to ask God how He can help you.

God gave us emotions, but He also gave us the Holy Spirit to guide us with discernment on how to manage it. Healthy anger management is vital to your healing.

Be angry, and yet do not sin; do not let the sun go down on your anger, ²⁷ *and do not give the devil an opportunity.* Ephesians 4:26-27

Survival may depend on how you handle your anger. Every war has its battlefield, some which may leave you without cover and vulnerable to the enemy. Don't give the enemy any kind of advantage.

<u>Prayer</u>
God, I need your help right now to deal with the wounds that have hurt me. Take my anger and bring me wisdom on how to speak, in Jesus' name. Amen.

Divorce to Healing: Day 5
Obedience

Everyone hates being told what to do. "What right does so and so have to give me advice and telling me how to live my life? They have no idea what I am going through….You're not my mom!!!"

One of the hardest things for people to accept is advice, yet sound, biblical advice is life-changing. All of the best advice will ultimately drive people back to one thing…obeying God.

Too many people want microwave answers to slow-cooker issues. They want to get immediate relief for the pain that took months or years to create.

You have to get real and realize that if your way worked, you would not be in the situation you are in. Free will on the other person's part may play a big part of that, but realize that you had a hand in the matter too.

They are not 100 % at fault, if you are willing to be honest.

In this world, obedience can be misinterpreted as control, manipulation, or fear. In God's world, obedience means boundaries, protection, and love. When you live obedient to God's direction, you will feel the safety that only He can give.

Do you not know that when you present yourselves to someone as slaves for obedience, you are slaves of the one whom you obey, either of sin resulting in death, or of obedience resulting in righteousness? Romans 6:16

When you choose to be disobedient to God's life-giving direction, you are choosing to be a slave to the way of the world, which results in pain and hurt. Being obedient to God will not be easy, but it will bring you the healing you need.

<u>Prayer</u>

God, today I choose to obey your Word and the leading of the Holy Spirit. Help me to stay strong each day as I follow You, in Jesus' name. Amen.

Divorce to Healing: Day 6
Choices

"It doesn't really matter, right? I am an adult and I can do whatever I want. Trashing their vehicle would make me feel SOOOO much better!!"

Most people never realize that their choices in life have consequences. Too bad they find out when it is too late. Have you met someone like that? Are you there yet?

So many people just go through life doing whatever feels good or what someone else tells them to do. When was the last time they stopped and thought about what the consequences would be to their actions?

Good parents stop their kids before they touch a hot stove. Kids may not realize it, but it is painful!! As parents, our job is to protect our kids because we know what will happen if we don't. God wants to protect you in the same way.

God gave you a brain, USE IT!!

The school of Hard Knocks is just that, HARD!!! It hurts and it hurts more than just you. Life is not all butterflies & unicorns. Don't make it harder than it already is.

God created you with a conscience and you know what is right from wrong.

There is a way which seems right to a man, but its end is the way of death. Proverbs 16:25

Don't make choices based on how you feel. Don't trust emotions that are especially active at this time in your life. Weigh out what can happen before doing something that you could very possibly regret in the future.

<u>*Prayer*</u>
God, help me to make the choices that will not bring more pain and suffering. Give me the courage to make the correct decisions, in Jesus' name. Amen.

Divorce to Healing: Day 7
Loneliness

People who are naturally loners are probably wondering what the problem is, yet we all need belonging and community to regulate our emotions and feelings.

God created us to be a part of each other's lives. He created us for community and to give and receive love through those around us. As great as Adam was, he was not complete until Eve showed up.

Living lonely is hard. It is really hard. It hurts and causes us to rethink our motives. It drives us to do things out of desperation. It also is very misunderstood.

Being lonely and being alone are two TOTALLY different things. Being alone means nobody is with you. Being lonely is not being connected to anyone. How many times have you been in a room full of people, but feel totally alone? That is loneliness, not aloneness.

The struggle of loneliness is to learn to get and stay connected to people, especially those that speak life and wisdom to you. Beat loneliness with one phone call and one get together at a time. Make time for others to give you encouragement and invest time into helping you battle loneliness.

Be strong and courageous, do not be afraid or tremble at them, for the LORD your God is the one who goes with you. He will not fail you or forsake you. Deuteronomy 31:6

You are never alone. God is always with you!! If you need to pump yourself up anytime, repeat what God gave me at my lowest time – "Jesus and I are movin' on!!" You can't go anywhere that God is not already there. He has been waiting.

Prayer
God, help me to know more each day how wonderful it is to always have you by my side and others to come along side when they do, in Jesus' name. Amen.

Divorce to Healing: Day 8
Perspective

Have you ever had a day where you even wondered why this or that caused you to just lose it? Why can't an 11 year old daughter remember to grab her lunchbox when she gets out of the car making me drive back to school and interrupting my day?

Yes, things happen. When it comes to marriage and divorce, we usually have more questions than answers. So much happens that we seem to live in a state of ongoing heartache. You will never get all of your questions answered, so let's talk.

Have you ever climbed to a very high point, like to a mountain top or a lookout on vacation? It is amazing. You can see in all directions until you see the curve in the earth. It makes all of the things you left below seem so small.

Just like all of our questions, pains, emotions, and stress, a different perspective allows you to refocus on what really is important in life. It gives you a chance to see things from a different angle and give you a new perspective.

Does it mean that everything down below changes? Not at all. It just looks different. Does it mean that anything changes with your issues? No, but how you look at them does. It allows you to see other ways to address them.

And we know that God causes all things to work together for good to those who love God, to those who are called according to His purpose. Romans 8:28

Allowing others to speak life into you and letting God's Word give you a different set of 'eyes' allows you to see things about yourself that will make you stronger and bring forth a change in your approach to your healing.

<u>*Prayer*</u>
God, help me to see my struggles and hurdles through Your eyes and give me a heart willing to find Your perspective in all areas of my life, in Jesus' name. Amen.

Divorce to Healing: Day 9
Trust

"How will I ever be able to believe what anyone says ever again? Why can't people follow through with their promises and stay faithful? When will I be able to let go and allow someone into my life again after all that has happened?"

In our culture today, it seems that standing on principle and being a man or woman of your word is a lost attribute. Infidelity, lying, and back-stabbing are too common place and cause us to re-evaluate all of our relationships.

There comes a day when you need to finally deal with the wound created by a breach of trust. Only you will know when that is. Your relationships have enormous value and you need to bring value to them as well, slowly at first. Family and friends really want to help and that gives you a place to start.

Do we realize how much of our lives are affected by trust? Do we trust that the person driving towards us on the other side of the road will stay in his lane or that they will stop at the red light? Will the bus driver bring our child back today?

The level of trust you have for any person is in direct proportion to the amount of pain caused, and that is offset by the healing you have allowed to happen in you.

And those who know your name will put their trust in You, for You, O LORD, have not forsaken those who seek You. Psalms 9:10

We need to learn that trusting others does not mean we drop our guard and allow ourselves to be hurt. Trust is earned, not given. Trust in who is trustworthy. Human beings are not perfect, so give grace to others and learn to trust again.

Prayer
God, I pray that I can place my trust in You to guide me in learning to trust others again and that they give me grace as I heal in this area, in Jesus' name. Amen.

Divorce to Healing: Day 10
Forgiveness

"Really? really...?...?.. This is the last thing you are thinking about. That _____ doesn't deserve one more moment or thought. They can go to heck for all you care. Well, maybe not......"

There comes a time when things have gone wrong. Depending on where you are at in your healing process, you may or may not be ready to forgive. That is absolutely ok!!

Forgiveness is a singular, personal issue between you and God. The only part the other person plays in all of this is that they were the cause of it, yet they have nothing to do with you forgiving them.

Forgiveness is a choice, just like love. It is not a feeling. Only you can choose to forgive, for the health of yourself and for your relationship with God.

Not forgiving is like drinking poison and expecting the other person to die.

Forgiving someone for the wrongs and the pain they have caused you, does not mean what they did was ok. It doesn't mean that it doesn't matter or that things will get better. It doesn't mean forgiveness is deserved or due. Forgiving does not mean you forget. We are not God, we are human.

For if you forgive others for their transgressions, your heavenly Father will also forgive you. But if you do not forgive others, then your Father will not forgive your transgressions. Matthew 6:14-15

Choosing to forgive is like giving God permission to remove the bandage of offense from your heart, so that he can clean and start healing the wound.

<u>*Prayer*</u>
God, today I choose to forgive (_____) for (_____). I lay it at the foot of the cross and ask you to heal every part of me that is wounded, in Jesus' name. Amen.

Divorce to Healing: Day 11
Thankfulness

Some people may tell you to be thankful for ditching that zero, losing that ball and chain, etc. I challenge that notion. Being thankful for a divorce is as crazy as being thankful for an accident that causes injury or death. That is crazy!!

Divorce is an event in one's life that causes the ground to shake under their feet and question themselves, their judgements, and others. It also opens the eyes of a person to show them that no matter what happens, you have something left.

Even if you lose your marriage, spouse, kids, finances, house, job, car, etc.., you can still find many things to be thankful for. Depending on where you are in the healing timeline, just the ability to still be alive and reading this is a start.

When you stop and take a full inventory of what is left, it will look drastically different than what you had, but you may finally realize things you never gave a moment's thought to before: supportive friends/family, life, being able to walk & talk and have hair on your head. How many people wish they had what you have?

During difficult times, most people find it hard to see all of the things they are thankful for. Write down on a piece of paper at least 10 things and put it someplace where you will see it every day, like a mirror or your bible.

in everything give thanks; for this is God's will for you in Christ Jesus. 1 Thessalonians 5:18

When you can see and be thankful for the things you still have left, it will allow you to realize that things aren't as bad as they could be. Make it a daily goal to add one new thing to be thankful for to your list. Mine is that you are here today.

Prayer

God, let me see your blessings and be thankful for what I have. You fed thousands with 5 loaves and 2 fish. I thank you for what I have now, in Jesus' name. Amen.

Divorce to Healing: Day 12
Confusion

"Why did they leave? Why ruin our family? What did I do wrong?" Very few life events will ever measure up to divorce when it comes to confusion.

There are so many thoughts that come into our mind. Most of them are a waste of time and are only rooted in fear. Fear has been described as F.E.A.R. False Evidence Appearing Real.

Negative thoughts about the future virtually never come to pass and all it does is rob you of your peace. When you dwell on what MIGHT happen in the future, you take your eyes off of dealing with the present.

Just know that you don't need to live a life of confusion. You need to take control of what you have control over, and leave the rest to God. Have faith that He will bring clarity to your mind so that your emotions can be brought into check.

Find yourself godly people to counsel you. Whether it is emotional, financial, or situational issues you are struggling with, find someone that you can talk through your thoughts with that can bring light to them.

God gave us faith to allow Him to fight our battles for us, especially those that we have no idea how to handle. He is the one that brings peace in spite of confusion.

for God is not a God of confusion but of peace, as in all the churches of the saints.
1 Corinthians 14:33

When you find yourself unsure of why, reach out to the One who has all of the answers. They may not be the answers you want, but they will be the right ones.

<u>*Prayer*</u>
God, teach me to come to You for the answers to all the questions I have and give me the strength to have faith in You to guide my thoughts, in Jesus' name. Amen.

Divorce to Healing: Day 13
Acceptance

Even before a divorce happens, our feeling of acceptance can be shattered. "Why am I not good/pretty/handsome/rich/nice/blessed enough for them to love me just the way I am?"

The feeling of not being accepted shakes our belief in ourselves and tears down our self-images causing us to question our place in this world.

Too many times, we think acceptance and approval goes hand in hand. They are two totally different subjects.

You do not need to approve of someone's sins and destructive behavior to accept them as a human being and someone that needs our love and forgiveness.

When you accept someone else, you agree to not allow other people's issues to change how you value them as a person.

When we become parents, we accept our children even though they spend most of their first days crying, pooping, and sleeping. They cannot validate us, yet we accept them because we love them.

Especially now, we all need acceptance and the best way to receive acceptance, is to accept others, good or bad.

Therefore, accept one another, just as Christ also accepted us to the glory of God. Romans 15:7

Our acceptance is determined by the value of the one giving it, and God thinks you are worth great value. He accepts you, no matter what anyone else says

<u>Prayer</u>
God, help me to accept others while I grasp how deeply You accept me, in Jesus' name. Amen.

Divorce to Healing: Day 14
Feelings

How do you feel right now? Did you just wake up and not had your coffee yet? Is it the end of your day and you are wondering how you can continue just one more day? Have you reached for this page to validate your feelings?

During these 31 days, you will probably experience more variations of feelings than you ever knew you could feel. This is normal and expected. Divorce is not something you are ever expecting or planning to happen. And it will be ok.

God gave us emotions and feelings so that we can function here on earth. Without them, we are just robots moving day by day without any way to truly be human. Jesus had feelings, greatest of that was love for His Father and for you!!

Don't beat yourself up because you feel a certain way. Just know that it is ok and you can use every feeling as a chance to have a deeper relationship with Jesus. Tell Him know how you feel. He will help you use it to grow towards becoming complete and whole.

The Psalms are filled with verses about David's feelings towards his enemies and his situations. He also had deep feelings towards God, sometimes praise and sometimes total despair. You are not alone in that.

Therefore let us draw near with confidence to the throne of grace, so that we may receive mercy and find grace to help in time of need. Hebrews 4:16

Feelings are there to help bring understanding, protection, and guidance, yet they are not meant to control us. Let them help you draw closer to Jesus daily.

Prayer

God, no matter how I feel, I choose to allow you to guide and direct me by Your Holy Spirit instead of allowing my feelings to control me, in Jesus' name. Amen.

Divorce to Healing: Day 15
Bitterness

Have you ever had the experience of falling into quicksand? I never have, but I have heard that the only way to survive is to stop struggling and lay flat on your back with your limbs extended like you are floating. Stop fighting it. Surrender.

One of the hardest things we must ever do is to learn to forgive. It is not something that comes easy to us, but it is vital for our healing.

Unforgiveness is a poison we drink thinking it will harm someone else, but all it does is harm us. When we allow experiences against us to continually affect us negatively, we have continued to allow that person to control our well-being and healing. Don't let that happen to you.

I know right now you may not be ready to forgive, and that is understandable. If you refuse to deal with it, a root of bitterness will be growing within your soul that grows every day, getting deeper with every passing moment. Every day you ignore it just makes the removal of the root that much harder and harmful.

If you see a weed in your garden, do you let it stay there? Did you know that it is robbing nutrients and water meant for the fruit God is trying to grow in your garden? Every day you wait, the root grows bigger and its seeds will eventually affect the whole garden, if you don't deal with it.

See to it that no one comes short of the grace of God; that no root of bitterness springing up causes trouble, and by it many be defiled. Hebrews 12:15

If you are not ready to forgive today, just make a decision to move towards that more and more every day. God will help you and He will give you a heart to do it.

<u>*Prayer*</u>
God, let no seed of bitterness take root in me and may I realize how I must forgive others to keep my spiritual garden healthy and growing, in Jesus' name. Amen.

Divorce to Healing: Day 16
Pain

Wounds cause pain. Wounds are proof of an attack against us physically, mentally, or emotionally. Blood and tears are released to alert us to the wounds and also to be the first steps in the healing process.

Sometimes people want to dismiss the pain. I know as a man myself, I do not want to show my weakness, especially in front of my wife and children. I need to stay strong and be an example of strength at this time.

Did you ever wonder why we feel pain? What would it be like if we could not feel it? We would never know when we have been wounded and need to heal.

Pain killers are used when the body is unable to cope with the physical pain. Just like that, the Holy Spirit is the pain killer for your soul. You get no relief unless you find the correct pain killer to handle your pain…God!!

Jesus gave us the answer for pain. He allows us to feel it to draw our attention to the wounds in our lives and also provides the salve for the soul. Don't just curl up and feel the pain, get some relief.

Pain also leaves scars. I describe a divorce like open heart surgery. When you are healed, your heart will work again, but at the cost of a huge scar on your chest. Eventually the wound heals, but it leaves a scar to remind you of the pain and to show you that pain only lasts until you are healed

He heals the broken-hearted and binds up their wounds. Psalms 147:3

Realize that your pain is temporary and that Jesus will heal you, if you go to Him.

Prayer
God, through the pain I will trust that you will bring the healing that I need to heal fully and completely, in Jesus' name. Amen.

Divorce to Healing: Day 17
Yearning

Some of the most difficult times in our lives are those that cause us to desire things we cannot have. I want my 20 year old, 185 pound physique back. I may lose the weight, but something tells me I will never be 20 years old again.

We all yearn for something or someone. During separation and divorce, we yearn for our relationship with the person we have lost, when it was so happy and life-giving to both.

Feelings of longing for a relationship we used to have or the possibility of a new one, is not wrong and you should not feel bad about that. Just be realistic with your feelings.

Yearn for that which you can attain - a healed heart and a renewed soul. Reach to acquire the help you need to get you there, such as professional help or pastoral care. Give yourself a chance.

Growth comes through stretching for more than you have now. Just like a rubber band, by stretching it out, it actually expands when it retreats leaving it able to do more next time.

Take time to yearn, but for what matters and for what will bring you the healing and wholeness you need to move forward.

Or do you think that the Scripture says in vain, "The Spirit who dwells in us yearns jealously"? James 4:5

There is someone who does yearn and longs jealously for a sincere relationship with you; Jesus. Take time to let him show you what a real loving relationship is.

<u>*Prayer*</u>
God, may my heart and soul be filled with Your love so completely that I can feel how jealously you yearn for us to spend time together, in Jesus' name. Amen.

Divorce to Healing: Day 18
Baggage

Whatever you bring into a new relationship that hasn't been dealt with in a healthy manner and been healed is similar to a hard-shelled Samsonite with a bum wheel.

If you are wounded, get healing. If you are confused, get wisdom. If you are bitter, get forgiveness. Don't carry it on to the next relationship.

How would you feel if your son or daughter came back from college for a visit and brought you 3 extra bags filled with rotten food from the dorm fridge? Why didn't they just deal with this by getting rid of it before they came to see you?

Now, think about a possible new relationship you may have in the future. Would you like them bringing you bags of bitterness, pain, spite, anger, addiction, or any number of things? Is that fair to you?

When we carry things with us into our future that were meant to stay in the past, it causes us to force it upon someone else that does not deserve to have to deal with it.

Does it mean you can't move on until you deal it? No, but you will never be healed and whole until you do. Would you want to jump into a leaky boat with only some of the holes plugged or repaired? You will still sink.

let us also lay aside every encumbrance and the sin which so easily entangles us, and let us run with endurance the race that is set before us. Hebrews 12:1

Have you ever wondered what happens to the bags you leave behind? They sit going around in circles until they are collected and destroyed. Let them be. You have places to go and it will only hold you back.

<u>*Prayer*</u>
God, right now I choose to let go of_____ and I refuse to go back to pick it up ever again. May it always remain in my past, in Jesus' name. Amen.

Divorce to Healing: Day 19
Grief

For so many people, it is hard for them to express their feelings while trying to encourage you during this difficult time. They mean well, and for the most part they are just doing what they can. At least they are trying.

I know how you feel. I have been there, yet I survived. Twice. It hurts.

It has been said that divorce is worse than death, because if children are involved, you will probably have to deal with the other person for many years to come even after the divorce. At least in death, you have some permanent closure.

Take your time and do not rush the grieving process. Make time for the ugly cry. Allow yourself to breakdown with those that are closest to you. Be real.

It is not selfish to allow yourself a reasonable time to mourn. Everyone is created differently and you are not a robot.

I remember my brother told me just two simple things when I told him about my situation. He said that he was there for me, no matter what and that he would not push himself on me but give me the time and space to work through my feelings. It really allowed me the space and also the support that I so desperately needed.

More than any other time in your healing process, having a small and tight group of family and friends that will just be there for you will be a great relief and help.

My soul weeps because of grief; Strengthen me according to Your word. Psalms 119:28

You grieve when you lose something or someone of value, and by grieving you are honoring that relationship. If it doesn't hurt, did you not place any value in it?

<u>Prayer</u>
God, I am hurting right now. Hold me in your arms and give me the strength to make it day to day as I let You heal my heart completely, in Jesus' name. Amen.

Divorce to Healing: Day 20
Boundaries

Remember when you were growing up and your parents had a list of demands (do nots) a mile long that just killed all the fun? What did they know? Where they just trying to be difficult?

What makes you feel safe and secure? Armed bodyguards help, but not at 35,000 feet in a nosedive. Physically speaking you can do lots of things to lower your risk, but these only protect the body. You can also do that to protect your soul as well.

Our soul (mind, will, and emotions) is as safe as a newborn baby, unless we fortify it with safeguards and protections that allow us to live safe and keep out that which wants to harm us.

By providing a healthy protective wall away from things that will only continue to hurt us, Godly boundaries protect us and give us a place to live where true healing can take place. A body cannot heal while still on the battlefield.

Search out those actions that hurt you and reject those things that God wants you to stay away from so that He can protect you. Sowing seeds of wrong living will only cause you to reap more pain and struggle. It may even kill you.

The amount of land (your heart) you give God control over is the amount He can protect. Let Him have it all. He won't heal the land (your heart) which you refuse to surrender. It is like letting a heart surgeon only given permission to operate on the left half of your heart.

…so that it may go well with you, and that you may live long on the earth. Ephesians 6:3

See how safe boundaries and actions can change your life like nothing else.

Prayer
God, show me those safe and secure boundaries for my life that will allow me to heal completely and walk in the freedom of wholeness, in Jesus' name. Amen.

Divorce to Healing: Day 21
Hope

With all you have already gone through and so much more you may still be facing, do you ever feel like it is just too much? Why bother? Will you ever have peace?

The answer is yes or no. That may sound strange, and it is meant to cause you to pay attention, because this could make or break you. And I want it to be yes!!

The answer is yes, if you can be honest with yourself. Know that you need help and get it. Know that you need others around you that speak life into you and don't lead you into destructive thoughts or actions. Know that God is the answer!!

The answer is no, if you just decide to spend your time hating others, being angry, not forgiving, and just doing what feels good. Know that these things will just give you more pain and struggle, causing you to spiral towards a life of less than great.

Honestly, the only real answer I give to people who ask my advice is to seek Jesus with everything you have and follow Him. Any other advice is from a sorry man who has failed twice at marriage, yet found complete healing and peace with just that advice. Hope is there for you, if you choose it.

People's stories of survival in dire situations seem to get boiled down to hope. They realized that without hope, they would never be rescued. It even sometimes led them to discover a new plan or strategy to get them out of their tragedy.

"For I know the plans I have for you," declares the LORD, *"plans to prosper you and not to harm you, plans to give you hope and a future."* Jeremiah 29:11

There is always hope. Hope is all around you, just like the air you breathe. Every time you breathe in, air comes in. Open your heart and let hope in!!

<u>*Prayer*</u>
God, I need You now!! I need you to be the hope in my life and to show me how to live each day hoping for a greater life, in Jesus' name. Amen.

Divorce to Healing: Day 22
Comparison

If it's not bank accounts or looks, then it is cars or relationships. We compare costs, features, and usefulness for almost everything. When it comes to where you are now in your healing process, don't do it.

I know you wonder if the other person in your ex's life is a better cook, lover, provider, or parent. It is human nature, but that is not God's nature.

When we compare ourselves to others, it is really just us comparing our worst to their best, our lack to their abundance, our pain to their joy. I know, because I did it too.

Why give someone else that has negatively affected you control over your thoughts and image of yourself? What right do they have? Only the right that you give to them by allowing yourself to play a game of comparison that you cannot win.

Why not compare your situation to someone laying in a bed dying of cancer? How about the millions of starving and abused children all over the world, even in America? Even that is pointless, unless you need to get a reality check.

You are special. You have gifts and talents that nobody else on the earth has ever had or ever will again, in the way you were created. Only you can do what God has created you to do, and no one can compare to that, even if you are hurting.

Wisdom and identity in truth will allow you to move beyond comparing.

For wisdom is better than jewels; And all desirable things cannot compare with her.   Proverbs 8:11

You are becoming someone who will have no equal. You will be able to give help and wisdom to others because of what you are learning now. Get ready.

<u>Prayer</u>
God, help me to not compare my weakness to other's strengths. Let me know that you never compare me and that you always love me, in Jesus' name. Amen.

Divorce to Healing: Day 23
Regret

One very difficult thing you must do is fight the urge to live with regrets. We have all done and said things that we wish we would have handled differently. That is just life and being human.

Letting the past cloud our present does nothing to help us heal and it robs us of precious energy and time. It only prolongs the process.

It is one thing to analyze those actions of our past that have caused us pain, whether it was our fault or not. It is another thing to keep rehashing over and over again what should be handled and dealt with, then left in the past.

View those regretful situations only for the good they can bring: gaining wisdom to understand and eventually helping to encourage or share with others when they may eventually be dealing with the exact same thing.

One of my greatest regrets that I had to handle was not knowing how to communicate. I blamed it on many things, but ultimately I needed to learn how to communicate and realize that it was ok to just tell people how I felt.

By moving forward and working through whatever regrets you may still have, you will start to put the pieces of the healing puzzle together.

For the sorrow that is according to the will of God produces a repentance without regret, leading to salvation, but the sorrow of the world produces death. 2 Corinthians 7:10

Use the pain of the past to prepare you for your future. Learn and then let go. You can't do that if you don't stop looking in the rear-view mirror of life.

<u>*Prayer*</u>
God, help me to have no regrets for deciding to let you handle my life and doing what is right in Your eyes, in Jesus' name. Amen.

Divorce to Healing: Day 24
Trusting

One of the biggest failures in divorce, usually the greatest factor, is a destruction of the trust built between you and your spouse. Usually another person has been involved in some way. Faith is shattered when trust is broken by another.

People may give you every reason to grab a knife/gun/tank/nuclear bomb and just make sure that it will never happen again. As tempting and fulfilling it may make you feel, spending the rest of your life in jail on top of all of this is not recommended, let alone desired. Just don't do it.

Most people tell you that trust can never be restored, but that is untrue. Many people have invested in preserving their marriage, so it can be done. Although a vast majority have not, it can and it takes two willing and totally unselfish people working through much pain and wise counsel to accomplish it.

When you start to come to grips with things, don't allow yourself to assume the blame for another person's sin and mistakes. Choices have consequences.

The way to develop trust again is a long, hard road. Make sure you get help from those qualified to guide you correctly towards a real healing in that area.

You will be able to trust again, but you must never allow your trust in a human being be greater than your trust in the only One who is fully trustworthy.

"Behold, God is my salvation, I will trust and not be afraid; For the LORD GOD is my strength and song, And He has become my salvation." Isaiah 12:2

Trust is not given, awarded, or bought. It is earned only by the one who is proven trustworthy. After you fully trust Jesus to heal you, He will help you trust again.

Prayer
God, I desperately need Your help to be able to trust You more each day for everything. I choose to trust you instead of man, in Jesus' name. Amen.

Divorce to Healing: Day 25
Responsibility

We have so many things that we are responsible for from kids and family to work and relationships. It can really feel daunting, especially when you struggling with divorce and all that entails.

It takes a lot of wisdom to know what is truly important, what can wait, and what really matters in the long term. It takes more than what we have in our feeble minds to figure this all out. Help is on the way.

If you are not an organized person, get organized. Use a calendar and write things down, especially your daily to-do lists. It will help you keep track and provide direction on what to get done. You would be amazed how scatter-brained you will feel during a time of tragedy, which is exactly what divorce is.

Make time to invest in your own well-being like quiet time, devotion, and stress relief.

Take time to see the value in your kids, your job, and your relationships.

Don't use these things to isolate yourself from people or God, but use them to grow closer to Him and to gain the strength you need to continue on with life.

Now, handle your matters in a way that is responsible. Take the high road. Give of yourself to others, even though you may not have strength to do it. Be a light and a rock for those that desperately need you, because you matter to them.

Arise! For this matter is your responsibility, but we will be with you; be courageous and act." Ezra 10:4

You have so many responsibilities, and it is a good thing. You have been trusted with so many things like being a mom or dad, a friend, and a blessing to others.

Prayer

God, give me the strength and wisdom to live responsibly and in such a way that others will see how you have helped heal and lead me, in Jesus' name. Amen.

Divorce to Healing: Day 26
Patience

Why is it so hard to wait? Is it because we have become a culture of instant microwave gratification? The world demands more, bigger, faster, now!

With modern technology, even if a child is born earlier than the normal development time of nine months, we can do what we can to bring full development along. It is not without its' own challenges.

How long will it take? How perfect do you want your healing?

There is a perfect time for you to have a fully healed and whole heart again. If you want a life that is allowed to move forward in joy, peace, and wholeness, you will need to allow whatever time it takes. Everyone is different and every healing process takes time, sometimes longer than others.

If you rush into another relationship, engage in destructive behaviors, and try to shortcut the process, your healing will be full of developmental and possibly life-long challenges that you will end up regretting. It is not worth it.

Just like after planting a seed, it depends on the quality of the seed, the amount of water, how far it is buried, among other factors that determine what kind of harvest you will receive. That little seed will not care if we want it right away.

Yet for this reason I found mercy, so that in me as the foremost, Jesus Christ might demonstrate His perfect patience as an example for those who would believe in Him for eternal life. 1 Timothy 1:16

Just like it still takes 9 months for a baby to fully develop, God has allowed his perfect timing to bring forth the perfect healing in you. Don't rush perfection.

<u>Prayer</u>
God, please help me to calm down and allow You the time to fully and completely heal all of the broken pieces left in my life, in Jesus' name. Amen.

Divorce to Healing: Day 27
Reconciliation

An amazing number of people who are separated or divorced have seriously considered and desired to reconcile, even if the other person has moved on with a new relationship and even married. It is more than understandable.

But for those of you wanting to throw your phone, tablet, or computer across the room towards me, I know there are a large group who are in the Good Riddance gallery for many valid reasons.

I would like to encourage those that have a sincere and Godly desire to allow God to bring you back to your first love; however, make sure they are not married and get with a pastor or counselor who will help you. To everyone, I say this:

Reconcile yourself and what you can of the relationship. Especially if children are involved, you need to be able to be civil and able to co-parent well so that it will cause less long-term damage to your relationship with them. You and your ex will always be their parents, and both are needed. Work together to make it happen.

Mutual friendships may need to be healed as well. They may not know what to say or do and often really don't want to lose you both as friends.

When you can be cordial and polite to those that have hurt you, you will be able to give an amazing testimony of how your healing is making you whole.

Now all these things are from God, who reconciled us to Himself through Christ and gave us the ministry of reconciliation... 2 Corinthians 5:18

Reconciliation is more about bringing people back into fellowship and civility than about returning to something you had in the past. Do it for your wholeness.

<u>*Prayer*</u>
God, whether our relationship can ever again include us being married I ask that You help to bring forth a mutual friendship between us, in Jesus' name. Amen.

Divorce to Healing: Day 28

Shame

When you saw the title for today, how did it make you feel? What did you think of that was negative? Was it about something you did or said?

Many things cause us to feel shame, to feel condemnation, or to feel less than perfect. Wrong thoughts and actions always have the worst waiting for us right before that corner of revelation, when we finally see what is not right.

Examine what others may be saying about you, but only to the extent that you can evaluate your thoughts and actions to bring forth positive growth. Don't allow them to continue to use it as a way of control. Take steps to right any wrongs, and then realize you were meant for better and to be better. Now go be better.

You do not need to live in a situation or a life filled with regret over things that have happened in the past. Consequences may follow, but you can get through them. Learn new life skills and communicate to others that things are new in you and that you are moving on in a positive manner to all God has for you.

Do you think the woman at the well felt shame? With all that Jesus knew about her, He brought revelation in her own spirit that her past was not right. What happened next? He showed her love and forgave her so she could tell live free.

So many more days lay ahead of you and you have so much more life to live. Don't spend one more day feeling shame and guilt. Do something about it now.

Be diligent to present yourself approved to God as a workman who does not need to be ashamed, accurately handling the word of truth. 2 Timothy 2:15

When you spend time in the Word of God, you will gain the strength and wisdom to move past all of your feelings of less than healed and whole.

Prayer

God, help me to live my life so I will not feel shame for any reason while I live more upright each day, in Jesus' name. Amen.

Divorce to Healing: Day 29
Evidence

The cop shows on TV and the local law enforcement are not the only ones who have to handle evidence. Searching, collecting, and examining evidence happens whenever something tragic happens, but there are so many ways to use it.

Evidence can convict and exonerate. It can lead and it can confuse. The person handling the evidence is the one who largely determines how best to use it, but it may not be the whole truth.

You are in the process of healing, and in that process there are pieces of the tragedy that shine a light on what happened. There will also be evidence of healing and that is where I want to spend the rest of our time.

What do you see in yourself that has learned from your past, good and bad? Have you realized those thoughts, words, and deeds that have brought you to this point and how they are impacting your life today? Learn from the bad, but dwell on those things that you see that are good. Make a list of the good ones!!

At your lowest point, did you ever think you would have been able to do some of the things you are able to do now? (i.e. keep the kids alive, communicate better, handle finances, enjoy your quiet time, remember to take out the trash, etc..)

So many little things all the way up to the big things are improving daily, even if you do not see it yet. Each day you wake up, you are one day closer to your healing and one day closer to the blessings God has for you.

Now faith is the assurance of things hoped for, the conviction of things not seen. Hebrews 11:1

Have faith!! Tomorrow will be better.

Some days may not, but add them up!!

Prayer

God, may the evidence of my healing be revealed to me day by day so that it may shine through me and so that others may also see your grace, in Jesus' name. Amen.

Divorce to Healing: Day 30
Peace

Do you long for peace? Do you pray for peace in your family and in your soul? Do you just need some peace and quiet? I may not be able to help with the quiet part, but if you have young kids, take it when you get it!!

There are those of us who need to just stop and give some peace to others. We need to end our wars and offer to at least be nice to one another. If that is you, for the love of all that is holy, please do it. Nothing rots a soul like a poisonous agenda looking to hurt someone else. To get peace, you need to start by giving it.

There are those of us who really just need peace, to make it through today. We need that quiet confidence that things are ok and are going to be better tomorrow. If that is you, do whatever you need to do to get it. Have someone watch the kids, call a friend or family member to talk, or get alone with God.

There will always be conflict, even in your greatest relationships. Don't let that discourage you. Through struggle comes strength, if you use it positively. Peace is more an attitude than a feeling. You can choose to live in peace.

When you strive to see people through God's eyes, you see them for who they really are; a child of God. Pray that they will see you the way God sees you.

Take the high road because in the end, the view is so much more peaceful.

Finally, brethren, rejoice, be made complete, be comforted, be like-minded, live in peace; and the God of love and peace will be with you. 2 Corinthians 13:11

Peace is not an absence of conflict, it is a quiet comfort in strength. Peace is not a lack of an enemy, it is the fullness of a relationship with the peace-maker, Jesus!!

Prayer

God, grant me peace today. Let me know how much You love me and allow my soul to be renewed, refreshed, and restored every day, in Jesus' name. Amen.

Divorce to Healing: Day 31
Joy

You may seriously question if you will ever have any real joy again. The answer is a resounding and whole-hearted YES!! Now, depending on your faithfulness to the healing process that God has for you, your joy may be great or small.

There are many kinds of joy: from a child's face or a playful puppy to a warm salty breeze bringing a stillness deep down in your soul. There is also an everlasting joy that only comes from knowing who's you are, not just who you are.

Don't settle for only joy in the company of others like the joy that you can manufacture by flying to a resort or finding your new mate. Strive for that joy that causes you to sleep well at night and look forward to what tomorrow brings.

Joy in the natural can be simple to attain and yet fast and fleeting. Joy in the spirit you don't even need to worry about. It is always there, encouraging and calling you into a greater life. It may even bubble up in uncontrollable laughter, too.

Look towards those things and people that make you joyful, not just happy or comfortable. There are those that when you leave spending time with them, you feel enriched in your soul and that is a joy builder.

I can explain it to you this way: if you have to think about creating joy, you are not there yet. It will come as you let God fill up that well of joy that has run dry in you.

For His anger is but for a moment, His favor is for a lifetime; weeping may last for the night, But a shout of joy comes in the morning. Psalms 30:5

Everybody wants and needs joy, but only the joy that comes from a healed and whole heart knowing how much they are loved by their Creator satisfies.

Prayer
God, may I feel the joy you have for me every day. Fill me with your love and peace so that your joy just rises up in my soul and heals, in Jesus' name. Amen.

Next Steps

This devotional is designed as a resource you can continue to use, over and over. Search the contents by subject to help strengthen you in a specific area when you are struggling or when you feel like you need to reinforce something you have already studied.

If you are not involved with a life-giving, bible preaching church, make it a priority. It will help you handle the isolation, receive pastoral care, and gain friendships through your fellowship.

Find a good small group geared around divorce recovery. My wife Christy and I led a great small group called DivorceCare (www.divorcecare.org) for years. We still have friendships with a lot of those people today. DivorceCare also has a daily email that you can receive that offers great encouragement and peace. I highly recommend it.

Focus on the Family is an organization that ministers help to the family in all areas, including divorce. They also have information that may help. (http://www.focusonthefamily.com/marriage/divorce-and-infidelity)

More information and resources can be found on the Divorce to Healing Blog at (https://divorcetohealing.wordpress.com/).

You can also follow us and join in community with others here:

Facebook: (https://www.facebook.com/divorcetohealing/

Twitter: (https://twitter.com/divorce2healing)

BE BLESSED!!

Divorce to Healing – Verses

Day 1:   Deuteronomy 4:30
Day 2:   Jeremiah 1:5a
Day 3:   Proverbs 21:2
Day 4:   Ephesians 4:26-27
Day 5:   Romans 6:16
Day 6:   Proverbs 16:25
Day 7:   Deuteronomy 31:6
Day 8:   Romans 8:28
Day 9:   Psalms 9:10
Day 10:   Matthew 6:14-15
Day 11:   1 Thessalonians 5:18
Day 12:   1 Corinthians 14:33
Day 13:   Romans 15:7
Day 14:   Hebrews 4:16
Day 15:   Hebrews 12:15
Day 16:   Psalms 147:3
Day 17:   James 4:5
Day 18:   Hebrews 12:1

Day 19:   Psalms 119:28
Day 20:   Ephesians 6:3
Day 21:   Jeremiah 29:11
Day 22:   Proverbs 8:11
Day 23:   2 Corinthians 7:10
Day 24:   Isaiah 12:2
Day 25:   Ezra 10:4
Day 26:   1 Timothy 1:16
Day 27:   2 Corinthians 5:18
Day 28:   2 Timothy 2:15
Day 29:   Hebrews 11:1
Day 30:   2 Corinthians 13:11
Day 31:   Psalms 30:5

All verses used were taken from the New American Standard Bible Copyright © 1960-1995 by THE LOCKMAN FOUNDATION All Rights Reserved.
http://www.lockman.org

BE BLESSED!!

Made in United States
North Haven, CT
17 October 2022